Your Purpose is not for you

A Step by step guide to understanding your purpose and understanding why it's not for you

Andre Notice

Copyright © 2021 by Andre Notice

All rights reserved. This book or any portion thereof may not be reproduced or used in any manner whatsoever without the express written permission of the publisher except for the use of brief quotations in a book review.

Printed in the United States of America

First Printing, 2021

ISBN: 9798476523321

Edited & Formatted by Show Your Success

Published by Andre Notice

Dedication

I dedicate this book to the woman that has been there from the start

The one that has my love, the one that has my heart

I work hard to make you proud. I work hard to make you pleased.

I made it my WHY to set you for life, place your mind at ease.

Mom, I dedicate this book to you and all that I do

I'm just getting started and God will see my goal through!

                I love you,
              Andre Notice

Table of Contents

Dedication iii
Intro vii

1. What is purpose? 1
   Creator vs. creation 2
   Destiny and destination 5
   The most important days of your life 8
   What does purpose look like? 9

2. Why don't we chase our purpose? 13
   Distractions 14
   Fear 16
   Upbringing 19
   Friends and family 22
   Jobs 24
   Conformity 25

3. What happens when we are not walking in
   our purpose? 29
   Identity crisis 30
   Job to job 33
   We settle 35
   We miss out on life-changing opportunities 36
   We fall into peer pressure 37
   Midlife crises 39

Table of Contents

4. How do you find your purpose?................41
   Pay attention................................42
   Exposure 46
   Reflecting on the past......................49
   Asking questions............................51

5. Why is our purpose not for us?..............55
   Your purpose is for others and the world....56
   Your purpose is for God.....................59
   Your position and purpose makes you more effective..............................61
   Life in one word............................62

6. How to confirm we are walking in our purpose......................................67
   Passion.....................................68
   People......................................71
   Pleasing....................................73
   Peace.......................................75
   Profit......................................77

7. What to do when you find your purpose?.....81
   Get to work!!!..............................82
   Plan..83
   Protect.....................................85
   Provide.....................................87

Conclusion....................................91
Acknowledgements: Superstar Supporters........93

Intro

If I were to ask you, where's the richest place in the world, where would you tell me? Would it be America, the world's capital of opportunity, rich with chances, opportunities, and avenues to succeed? Would it be Africa? With unlimited natural resources and elements in its mines filled with gold, diamonds, rubies, emeralds, sapphires, pearls, and such. Would it be China, the world's leader in population, holding about 18% of the people in the world's human life? What if I were to tell you the answer to this question is none of these places? What if I said the richest place isn't a city or country, or even a place you could visit? You see, I believe in what Dr. Myles Munroe said. To paraphrase what he said, "The richest place in the world is the cemetery because there, you will find books that were never written, businesses that were never started, practices that never opened, sermons never preached, motivational speeches never heard, paintings that were never painted, dreams that were never manifested, visions that were never realized, songs that were never sung....in the cemetery, you will find an unlimited number of unused ideas and untapped potential from generation to generation." Most people that have had the opportunity to breathe, live and die without ever discovering and understanding why they were even created to begin with. And so, I raise the question, did they really "live" or did they just exist? What about you in your life? Are you truly living? Do you have fulfillment in what you're doing, or are you just existing?

    I decided to write this book to change the narrative and the reality of most people living and dying without ever discovering why they were ever here. My passion and purpose are to see people live and leave a legacy. To see people reaching their full potential and constantly striving for more, for better, to be the best in their chosen field. So, in this book, I'll be asking a lot of questions. In fact, the title of each chapter is a question. That was done intentionally. Questions are what is needed to find purpose and grasp the concept of how vital it is to walk in it. In some of these questions, I may provide an answer. In others, they are thought-provoking questions for you to ponder and come to a conclusion of your own answer. This book is meant to be "purposeful" <-- see what I did there?

    I've learned through the years that, as humans, we learn best in four ways: rhythm, repetition, stories, and questions. So, in this book, I'll be using 3 of the 4 (repetition, stories, and questions). It would be most beneficial for you to review these concepts and ideas multiple times...read this book multiple times. Each time you read it, you'll unpack, uncover or understand something you didn't the previous time. Sometimes, it'll be so obvious you'll almost swear that what you see this time wasn't in the book the first time because you don't remember seeing it. Lol. You see, as you read, learn, grow, and mature, you begin to comprehend more, and you're more receptive to hearing new insight based on your new level of growth and maturity. Make it a point to work to grow as you seek to understand and comprehend the ideas posed in this book. Doing so will greatly increase your potential and increase the opportunity for you to find your purpose as you take the action steps outlined. To truly maximize your potential, take advantage of some free bonus material that I use with my clients, including my favorite thought-provoking quotes and scriptures at PurposeForMeBonus.com

And now, let us begin.

CHAPTER 1

What is purpose?

What is purpose?

I think it's vitally important to understand what I mean when I say purpose. What is the definition? Who am I speaking of? In this chapter, I will be talking about what I mean when I speak of purpose.

Creator vs. creation

So, what is purpose? Everything that is created, whether by man or by God, has a reason for being. Nothing was created for no reason at all. That reason for being is called purpose. Pick something... anything that you can name, point to, or reference. Anything and everything that is...was created. To be created, there must be a creator. That creator had a vision...a purpose for that creation. No thing was created just to be. Take a look around, even where you sit right now reading this book. The chair was created for you to sit, the bed to lay, the ink for us to write, the paper to be written on, the tablet to be read, TV for us to watch...everything that has come into being has a reason for its creation. That reason is called a purpose. Look around you and point to anything, and you may be able to see the purpose for each creation. You'll also notice that others benefit from its creation. Think about that for a second. A creator makes a creation, and we ALL benefit. All the underwater life in the ocean benefits from the sea being created. You and I benefit from automobiles that began with

What is purpose?

ONE person's vision to have a "horseless carriage" that others didn't believe would be possible at one point. Apple products were created with the vision of one individual to have a touch screen phone with a built-in computer and look how many millions of lives have been touched, transformed, made easier, and benefitted from one person's vision of innovation and creation. Both ideas (Apple products and automobiles) are now realities that were once just ideas in someone's head. When they began to act on these ideas, they weren't easily received or believed possible by others. That's another thing; sometimes, when you share your purpose with others, it's not always easily received. But we'll get more into that a little later. The point is, even those things were all created for a purpose that we all benefit from.

When you buy a new product (the creation), it always comes with an instruction manual from the manufacturer (the creator). That manual has specific instructions, dos, and don'ts for proper use of their product (its creation). Therefore, you know exactly why it was created, how it can be useful, and how to operate it. Just like all things were created for a purpose, it's no different for you and I. So, if we, as humans (the creation), want to find out our purpose, we need to turn to our manufacturer and creator (God) and His instruction manual for His creation, the Bible.

What is purpose?

As humans, we are created beings. Many believe the word "human" comes from the Latin word "humus," which means composed from soil, dirt, earth, or ground. The word "man" is defined as a "being," so when you put them together, you have "human," a being created from the dirt. Our human bodies are mere "shells" that temporarily house the real you. You are spirit, soul, and being. This is why when we die, they put our shells right back where we first started and where we were formed…in the dirt.

Then the Lord God formed a man from the dust of the ground and breathed into his nostrils the breath of life, and the man became a living being.
~ Genesis 2:7 NIV

The essence of God is not only omnipresent, meaning everywhere at all times, but He's also omniscient, meaning all-knowing. Consider this idea that God created each man, woman, and child for a specific purpose. He knows Everything about you, even before you made it here. God knew way ahead of time who would be your parents, how and when they would conceive you, and under what circumstance. Even though God doesn't control how you came into this world, He still knows you're going to make it here and how. Even if you were considered an accident by your parents, you are not an accident by God. Rest in that knowledge and accept the fact that God already knew you'd be here, and because He knew that, you are here for a reason. He designed a special purpose, path of direction, just for you. NO ONE else born before or after you can do what God created you (specifically) to do. Going throughout life without discovering and fulfilling that reason leaves an empty void within us. The question is, do you know what that one thing is, and will you fulfill it?

Before I formed you in the womb, I knew you, before
you were born, I set you apart
~ Jeremiah 1:5a

The first observation you may or may not see in this verse is that God takes credit for His creation. He says, "Before I formed you...". This is God reminding His creation that He is the Creator. Although we all came from our mother's womb, God still takes credit for His creation when saying, "I formed you." But He is also clear about stating that He knew us BEFORE we were even conceived. You are creation, created by the Creator for a reason...a purpose.

Destiny and destination

Your purpose is important because it gives your life meaning - it provides direction. I heard a quote from

Dr. Myles Munroe that I've never forgotten. He said, "Your reason for existence is called purpose, and when you can see it, it's called vision." I would have to agree. But how many people do you think have a vision for their life? How many people do you think really KNOW why they were created and run towards that as their life's goal? What percentage of people do you think wake up in the morning and get out of bed to do *more* than just work, pay bills and take care of their families? Why do YOU get out of bed?

When you get out of bed in the morning, how many times do you step foot outside your bedroom door and have nowhere to go? How about your house? How many times do you get dressed, get into your car, start the engine, put the car in gear, and have no destination in mind as to where you're going? I guarantee, unless you're joyriding or trying to clear your head, it isn't often. Your life is just as important. Many people...I would even argue MOST people are sitting in the driver's seat, steering the wheel of their lives, driving, and have NO destination other than that to work, pay bills, take care of family and obtain possessions. Some might even live to impress others. But they were...you were created for SO much more. You see, every time you get behind the wheel, you should have a set location, a destination. Let's take a moment to reflect on just what would happen if you were to just get in your car and drive...no destination. Eventually,

What is purpose?

you'd run out of gas. Then you'd find yourself on the side of the road, upset, uncomfortable, unhappy, pretty much unsettled in a situation you don't want to be in, and probably a situation you wouldn't have put yourself in if you knew where it would ultimately lead. Well, how many people are living their lives the same way: uncomfortable, unhappy, upset, and unsettled? See the correlation? "So, Andre, are you telling me if I had a clear purpose for my life, that I would have fulfillment in living for something?" YES!!! Absolutely!!! Your purpose is your destiny or, in this case, your destination. Once you know where you're going, you know what roads won't take you there. Now, don't mistake this for thinking you'll have a straight path there. Very few, if any, paths are straight, but better to know where you're going than not. While you're in a car, on your way anywhere, pay attention to where you're going and how you're getting there. Notice the windshield is in front of you. There's a reason that the windshield is 5x bigger than the rear-view mirror. That's not by accident. You need to see the road ahead. You need to see where you're going. Your body follows your eyes. What your eyes see is where you're going. How many steps could you take, walking in ANY direction, before you bump into something? Do you think you might eventually trip, fall, stumble, possibly even hurt yourself? Maybe even all the above. When you walk, it's natural to look where you're going. While you're alive, it should be natural to know where you're going, specifically. So, what *are* you looking at? Is it your purpose, mapped out in goals? If not, consider this idea: You cannot be what you cannot see. So, what are you looking at?

The most important days of your life

Have you ever paid attention to which posts received the most Likes, comments, and shares on social media? What are those posts usually about? I've noticed that the two main events that get the most attention on social media are: 1) when a new child is born, and 2) when a wedding has taken place or is being announced. The world rejoices at both events because they are of great importance. Both of these events display a new life, the start of something new and exciting. No matter what's going on in the world, no matter what chaos is taking place, these are very important events that the world continues to celebrate. They bring about joy, laughter, smiles, and cheer to all the hearts around the world.

I remember hearing another quote also from the late and great Dr. Myles Munroe. He said, "The two most significant days in your life are: 1, the day you were born. And 2, the day you figure out WHY." Your purpose is *why*. Once you are born, your possibilities are endless. You have the opportunity and the time to become whatever or whoever you want. Ideally, and in a perfect world, your parents and the school system should be probing your mind to engage in activities centered around you finding your purpose and then cultivating your gifts and talents to fulfill it. But unfortunately, that's not what we have in today's school system. Your purpose should be the reason you get up in the morning. You should wake up and be EXCITED, working to achieve something greater than yourself. So much greater that it outlives you. Your purpose should lead you into leaving a legacy! Your purpose should be that which you chase, far more than any job, profession or career, unless that career path encompasses your purpose. When it's all set and done, you can retire from your job, but you can never retire from your purpose.

What does purpose look like?

The fact that you are still here and breathing is a clear indication that you have not yet fulfilled that purpose for which you were created. It's also important to note that your purpose may not necessarily be a profession or job, but it can be something you do while *on* your job. Think of purpose more like a gift, or array of knowledge accumulated from your personal past experiences. Your purpose could be to take this newfound knowledge birthed from your past experiences and pass it on to a specific group of individuals that can benefit from it. While it's true that God wants the best for us and wants us all to be in good health and right standing, it's also true that circumstances arise. We placed ourselves in situations and others that happened to us through no fault of our own. But what if it didn't happen to us, but for us? What if that unfortunate situation was allowed to make us stronger? Remember, the Bible says that "ALL things work together for the good of those that love God and are called according to his *purpose." - Romans 8:28*. I take that to mean that even in your worst experience that you have encountered, even the one that you are ashamed of, God can turn around and make it for His glory. That experience has now become your story. Your story can be shared with others for His glory. But of course, you can't see that as you're living the experience.

One example of this could be the powerful story of Les Brown. Les grew up in an adopted family, as he didn't know his biological parents since birth. At school, he was labeled "DT" for "Dumb twin" and was also called mentally retarded. Les had a dream of becoming a disk jockey but never chased his dream due to the opinion of others. It wasn't until he came across one teacher who cared, did he gather the confidence to chase his dream. The teacher asked him to complete a task in the classroom, to which

What is purpose?

Les responded, "I can't, sir." The teacher asked, "Well, why not?" Les then told him, "Because I'm not your student, I'm 'DT' the dumb twin, and I'm mentally retarded." What the teacher said next would forever change Les's mindset, self-image, and life from this day forward. The teacher said, "Don't ever say that again. Someone's opinion of you does not have to become your reality." This statement changed the way Les saw himself and the world around him. He then told his teacher of his dream to become a disc jockey. The teacher encouraged him to practice, to prepare right now, every day to become a disc jockey. Les then replied, "But I don't have a job right now." The teacher said, "It doesn't matter. It's better to be prepared for an opportunity and not have one, than to have an opportunity and not be prepared." The teacher was instilling in Les the act of faith. Myles Munroe said, "Preparation is the highest act of faith. If you don't prepare, you don't truly believe.

As time passed, Les would have his opportunity, and he grabbed it. Les became a disc jockey. After having to sleep on the floor of an abandoned building, never knowing his parents, being held back a grade, no college training, being labeled "dumb twin" and mentally retarded, Les went on to having his own talk show and becoming the world's top motivational speaker. The past circumstances that he overcame inspired so many others. Les was able to motivate, inspire and encourage others *BECAUSE* of his past experiences, failures, and temporary setbacks. Your purpose is still waiting, despite what you've been through. You are still worthy of something great, regardless of what you've been through or what's happened to you. Utilize that to your advantage and know that your past does not dictate your future. It has only made you stronger because you're still here.

Chapter 2

Why don't we chase our purpose?

Why don't we chase our purpose?

In this chapter, we will be discovering reasons why we don't chase our purpose. After discovering what purpose is, we can clearly see how important it is to fulfill it. With it being so important, why don't more people take the time out to chase and seek it? What gets in the way of us taking time out to find out why we were even created? There are SO many reasons; we'll just discuss a few here.

Distractions

One of the reasons why we don't chase our purpose is because we're distracted. To find your purpose, you need to be focused and intentional about seeking to do so. Distractions rob us of our time, our energy, and our efforts that we can use in other areas. An overlooked reality about distractions is that we don't always realize that we are even being distracted. Sometimes we think that we are being purposeful with the things that distract us. Some of the things that we think are blessings are also disguised as distractions. Have you ever been in a relationship that did not serve you? If that relationship did not serve you in a positive light, it's possible it was distracting you from doing something that could have been beneficial in the long run. Distractions can take you in a whole other direction than where you intended when you first started. One of the biggest distractions in today's modern society would have to be social media. Social media robs us of so much time that we can place in other areas. Have you ever sat and wondered how much time you spent just scrolling through social media, reading comments, likes, shares, and just reading the content of other individuals? How much more focused and intentional would your life have been if you spent half of that time doing something that actually served you, whether it was reading your goals, writing your goals, or acting on something that would lead you to achieve those goals? Social media has been deemed one of society's biggest time killers. But just think about that for a second. Our greatest commodity in this life is time. Time is something that we can never give back, so why would you want to kill it? To be more focused and intentional about finding your purpose or achieving any other goal in your life, be mindful of how much time you direct to social media.

Another major distraction is television. In a quick Google search, according to the AC Nielsen company, the average American watches more than four hours of television per day. That makes up to 28 hours per week in front of the television. That is as much as a part-time job. Can you imagine spending 4 hours per day, 28 hours per week doing something that yields you no positive gain or return besides temporary, empty satisfaction and entertainment but is literally killing your time? Sadly as Americans, we are distracted by that which entertains us. We would rather be entertained than educated. In short, entertainment itself can be a major distraction. We ought to limit and be conscious of how much time we spend being entertained. I implore you right now to take a stance and be cognizant of how much time you're devoting to watching television and on social media.

> *"Dictate those distractions that deter you from your destiny and distance yourself with a determined discipline. Don't delay."*
> ~ Andre Notice

Fear

Fear is another obstacle that prevents people from finding their purpose. Many people break down fear into an acronym: *F*alse *E*vidence *A*ppearing *R*eal. If you agree with this acronym, then what you're saying is, fear itself is false; it's not even real in the physical realm. It's pure emotion or feeling. It's a feeling based on an unknown outcome of a *possible* future, especially if the future is not preferred by the person thinking negative thoughts. Fear is an emotion that comes after thought. Many things that we fear may not even come to pass; it's mainly in our heads. We literally make up things in our heads that don't serve us, and even worse, we mentally dwell on these things. We mentally rehearse negative outcomes in our minds which increase the chances of them coming to pass because what you think about, you bring about. We focus more on what we *don't* want versus what we *do* want. Because fear is such a strong emotion, people tend to put into action another acronym for fear: *F*orget *E*verything *A*nd *R*un. Everything including that which they want. Even that which was made for us to have, we run from. Fear keeps us from obtaining that which we tell ourselves and others we want.

Fear is an emotion. Emotion is energy in motion. Thought is energy. Every thought must yield a return or result in the spiritual realm. It has been known and said for years that thoughts are things (Prentice Mulford wrote a book entitled, "Thoughts are things."). That is because if you hold a thought long enough, in the spirit realm and over time, it will be manifested into the physical realm. The energy you place behind a thought becomes an emotion or energy in motion that we call *feelings,* just like fear. Once you know and understand it, you can make it a habit only to think thoughts that serve you in a positive light. It takes practice and consistency, but it can definitely be done. I believe that this is why God told us, through the Apostle Paul, to only focus on positive thoughts.

Why don't we chase our purpose?

> *Finally, brethren, whatsoever things are true, whatsoever things are honest, whatsoever things are just, whatsoever things are pure, whatsoever things are lovely, whatsoever things are of good report; if there be any virtue, and if there be any praise, think on these things*
> *~ Philippians 4:8*

The misunderstanding or ignorance of this leads people to living lives they are unhappy about because they are often thinking negative thoughts, which can also lead to fear. You cannot have faith and fear in the same place at the same time. You either have faith, or you have fear. Where there is fear, there is no faith.

Fear hinders us from moving forward because it focuses on the negative. It enables us to place obstacles in our minds that stabilize us and keep us stagnant. It is hard to take positive action while thinking negative thoughts. One way to overcome this is to take Robert Kiyosaki's advice and acronym for fear that outlines how to push through: *Fail Early And Responsibly*. You can only fail if you take action. It's ok to fail as long as you fail forward. So, feel the fear and do it anyway. During his graduation speech, Jim Carrey made a statement I'll never forget, in reference to watching his father not go for his dreams. His father settled for a mediocre job instead of stepping out on faith and he still failed. To that, Jim said, "You can fail at what you

DON'T want, so you might as well take a chance at what you love." Powerful.

Change your thoughts to change your life. Change to focussing on faith in what you DO want. Remember, you weren't meant to be stagnant; you were meant to grow, progress, improve. You were created to evolve continuously. To find your purpose, you must have faith in both yourself and in your Creator, God.

"For God hath not given us the spirit of fear; but of power, and of love, and of a sound mind"
~ 2 Timothy 1:7 KJV

Upbringing

Believe it or not, your upbringing and the way you were raised can play a MAJOR role in you reaching your purpose or not. Some households have specific cultures where you're expected to work in certain fields to be deemed "successful" by that family's standards. For instance, I remember hearing the story of the highly successful, multi-millionaire, Jay Shetty. Jay is a highly sought-after content creator and digital strategist with a massive online following. But in an interview with Tom Bilyeu, on his popular Impact theory YouTube channel, he tells the story of how growing up in his Indian household, you're expected to either be a doctor, a lawyer, or a failure. There's no other acceptable option. Deviating to any other field but these two, you would be considered a failure in the eyes of the family.

Can you imagine all the lives he's impacted and businesses he's changed would not have been if he fell in line with what his parents and family had in mind and what *they* deemed as "success?" Jay could've missed his purpose from falling under the "rules" of his upbringing. How about you right now in your life? Are you currently doing what you want to do because you want to do it? Or is it possible you had some outside influence based on your upbringing? Did your parents or family play a role in the decision for what you do now or used to do? Many people go through their lives and make decisions for the future based on what others wanted for them. Sometimes they feel obligated due to that parent being there, loving them, and providing for them. Other times they just don't want to let that parent down and have not learned how to tell them, "this is not what I want for me." It's not an easy conversation to have and many children are scared, thinking it can change the dynamic of their relationship or upset their parent(s). But you must be true to yourself. You can better help your parents as they get older when you're doing what you're supposed to be doing versus what you're tolerating. You'll have a better chance at operating closer to your

Why don't we chase our purpose?

full potential when you're walking in your purpose. It's possible Jay Shetty might have done well for himself working in the fields his family intended, but he might have sold himself short of the multi-millions he's earned. Also, the opportunity to impact so many other people and businesses. His life has also been fulfilling, as he's doing what he loves and enjoys. He made the choice to chase his purpose, not a paycheck.

How many other children in similar households have children that grow up to be just what mom and dad wanted for them, and they miss the mark on what they were created for because they didn't have the courage to do what Jay did? It takes an insane amount of courage to chase what you want, knowing you'll face ridicule, judgment, and possibly being alienated from your own family and those that love you. You also have to pursue it alone because the family will not support or finance your "rebellion."

How many teachers, doctors, lawyers, accountants, coaches, sales agents, nurses, etc., do we have in today's society of people working in these fields where they're not gifted or excited about only because it's what their family had in mind? Many of these individuals, unfortunately, miss their purpose and it often shows up in their work with how they speak to others. They are unhappy and unfulfilled and their results often reflect their work.

Friends and family

You win the lottery; you just found out the gender of your unborn child; you just got engaged; you just took a photo with your favorite singer. Someone just tried to steal your car in front of you. You just saw the funniest video that made your abs hurt from laughing...What's typically and naturally the first thing we do? We share it with others. We post it on social media. We immediately call a friend, we turn to the person around us, even if they're a stranger. It's really the main reason social media is so addicting. We're social beings, addicted to the feeling we get when we "share" and "post" what we've experienced because we want others to celebrate with us, laugh, cry, and feel and experience what we do and when we do. It's natural to be excited when a person finds out and begins to walk into or chase after their purpose. But when a person has a vision for their lives, only THEY can see it, no one else. When you make a decision to share your purpose and vision with others, know that everyone may not be as supportive as you hoped or expected. Many won't see it because they can't...and they weren't supposed to, at first.

One of my favorite Bible stories is the story of Moses and the people of Israel. In the Book of Exodus, God called out to Moses and told him what he was to do...He gave him his purpose. Moses was to guide the

Why don't we chase our purpose?

people from Pharaoh, in Egypt, and into the promised land. Moses now knew his purpose. But when you read the story, God didn't tell the people of Israel; He only told Moses. Remember, only YOU can see your vision, no one else. Moses' greatest challenge was getting the people of Israel to believe and buy into his purpose, even though it was for THEIR benefit. It literally took them 40 years to reach the promised land, not because the journey took that long in distance, but because they spent most of their time groaning and complaining and losing faith in what was ultimately for their benefit, but they couldn't see it. They couldn't see Moses' purpose, his vision. How much easier would this journey have been if everyone saw what Moses did? Your purpose is for you, but others can't see it. Many deter from chasing their purpose when they receive negative feedback from others: "You can't do that." What makes you think you can…?" "How are you going to…?" Hearing these questions and this response can be deflating and cause you begin to question if this was really meant for you. Many people don't find their purpose because they didn't believe in themselves as much as they believed in the opinions of others. They've allowed their friends, family, and others to influence their decision to chase their purpose. Don't allow this to be you.

Jobs

Believe it or not, jobs can be a big hindrance for people not walking in their purpose. While a job can be a blessing, it can also be a deterrent from what you are called and created to do, which gives you fulfillment. I recently talked with someone that mentors me in a specific area. This gentleman is great at what he does and has a gift to teach it well. He's enjoying the journey of teaching others what he's learned and seeing how they progress. But I remember him telling me how just a couple of years prior, he was working a job at a plant. The money was great, but it was taxing on the body, and he was forced to sacrifice rest and seeing his family. His job was slowly draining him from actually living and enjoying life. Life was meant to be joyful, fulfilling, and purposeful. But he wasn't able to impact, influence others or utilize his gift in teaching. In other words, his job was keeping him from his purpose and robbing him of the joy in life, even though it was providing for himself and his family. How many other individuals may be out there working a job that doesn't provide them any fulfillment beyond a paycheck? There are millions. This same gentleman received an offer to become a manager at the same location where he worked. He made the tough decision to decline the offer and actually quit his job. He came across another income-generating source and put all his time and energy into learning and becoming an expert in it. Though his wife and family did not understand and he kept failing, he continued to be consistent and persevere as an entrepreneur. Today, he is the main teacher for that growing company and enjoys waking up every day walking in his gift of teaching, all because he had the courage to leave his job and do what he felt was for him.

Conformity

What is the shape of water? Water takes the shape of whatever environment or object it is placed in. If you place water in a cup, it takes the shape of the cup. If you place water in a can, bottle, pool, jar, or car, it becomes and takes the shape of those objects. Water has no specific shape because it adapts, conforms, and becomes whatever it is surrounded by. In my personal opinion, conformity is also one of the biggest deterrents of people not finding their purpose. While it can be useful and important to adapt to your surroundings, it can be detrimental to *become* your surroundings, to the extent of losing yourself.

The difference is in losing a sense of self and individuality. Many people never find their purpose because they lack the courage it takes to be themselves, outside of the opinions of others. As toddlers and small children, we learned how to walk, talk and even shape our ideas from those around us. Our language and word usage comes from others, regardless if it was good or bad. Their influence played a major impact on not only what language we spoke, but even on the verbiage we used in that language...whether it was broken English, proper, or using a lot of profanity. Then, when we get to school, the first thing we want to do is "fit in." We, for some reason, want to be like everyone else. From what we wore, to how we spoke to those we chose to befriend, were all critiqued by others to assess who they thought we were. If a child is different, that child is usually thought of as awkward, odd, talked about, teased, bullied, and even isolated from the "in" crowd. No child wants to go through the ridicule and embarrassment of being alienated, so ever since we were in school, we did like everyone else and dressed like everyone else, regardless if they were followers or leaders. And since most people are not meant to lead, we end up subconsciously playing follow the followers. So, from birth to toddlers, children, and youth, we've conditioned ourselves to be like those we're surrounded by. We've become water. But were we supposed to be?

Two of the most successful individuals in modern society had the courage to do something different, opposite of outside opinions, ridicule, and judgment. They were Mark Zuckerberg and Steve Jobs and were both widely known to wear the same clothes every day. What would happen if any child did that in school? Could you imagine the embarrassment, jokes, and ridicule from other students that realize this? Kids don't stop to think or consider what that child may be going through, and they may not even care. Even an adult might even face tension from peers at the workplace for wearing the same thing every day. Eyebrows would be raised, snickering amongst others, and questions asked. To most, it just seems odd and awkward. Children and even adults make fun of what seems awkward without giving thought to the reason behind the action. But still, these men had the courage and self-confidence to be themselves and do what they felt was best for them. They were able to walk in alignment with the vision for their lives and created two of the biggest companies that have ever existed in American society. Their seemingly "odd" actions benefited them greatly by providing them additional headspace to think and form ideas for their life's creation. Not having to think about what to wear was just one less decision to be made, thus decreasing their chances of mental fatigue. They wanted their brains to operate at maximum capacity to fuel the decisions that mattered most to them. Because of their courage and discipline, their vision and creations have literally changed and shaped the world to something we never saw coming before, all because these gentlemen had the courage *not* to conform.

CHAPTER 3

What happens when we are not walking in our purpose?

What happens when we are not walking in our purpose?

What happens to a ship out on the ocean with no goal, no destination, or no captain at the wheel? I'd like to think that ship just goes from place to place; wherever the wind blows it is where it ends up. It may end up on some deserted island, spinning circles at sea, crashed into another boat, or even caught in countless storms until it eventually crashes and sinks. All things that move must have a clear direction and destination. YOU are a moving object or being. So, what direction are you headed if your movement isn't calculated, planned, directed, and intentional? What takes place if it's none of the above? Let's take a look at some of the possibilities of what can arise and what does as a result of those moving without a clear direction or purpose.

Identity crisis

I believe it can be hard to find out why you're created when you don't even know who you are. So many people place value in so many things outside of themselves because they can't seem to find the value *in* themselves. Every single one of us is valuable in our own way and right with our own unique set of skills and talents. But if you're unaware of these talents, chances are you're not using them. A big part of self-esteem comes from knowledge of self. While you are

What happens when we are not walking in our purpose?

not what you do, what you do plays a big part in who you are. Lack of self-confidence, self-awareness, and ignorance about oneself can often lead to placing value in other areas outside of themselves.

Having the *need* for a name brand, high-end, luxury items, holding up to a showy lifestyle, placing yourself in debt just to be seen in certain situations, areas, and environments, can all be a factor of having an identity crisis. Not knowing who you are can lead to you making an attempt to find your value in things. There's nothing wrong with having or wanting nice things, but that can be an issue when the desire for it is rooted in a foundation of trying to fill a void. Your value can be misplaced in what others find or deem as valuable. You can go through life constantly chasing material objects that give the illusion to provide a temporary sense of fulfillment but completely dismisses the real void that has yet to be addressed, identity.

Along with placing your value in things, another example of an identity crisis is placing your value in other people. You can place such high regard for another individual that you can find yourself subconsciously wanting to be like that person. Outside motivation is good, and being inspired by others is healthy, but wanting to be like others to the extent of wanting what they have and the lifestyle they perceive to have can lead to you missing a sense

What happens when we are not walking in our purpose?

of self and what's meant for you. You can miss out on what's for you by focussing too much on others

Tiffany works a regular nine-to-five. She's not happy about work and has to fight herself every day to get up just to get to work. Her job has been unfulfilling, her days seem to be long, and she's just over with the gossip that takes place on a regular day-to-day basis around the office. Tiffany loves kids, and unknown to her, her gift is in teaching. With minimal effort, she can easily place things together and explain things so that others understand and comprehend. Tiffany's friend, Melanie, is a realtor. She's been a licensed agent for almost 8 years and has worked her way to become a top producer. Tiffany watches how Melody is always winning real estate production awards, taking trips every month, and living a life of what Tiffany would call "The good life." Melanie drives her dream car and has just purchased a brand new half a million-dollar house where Tiffany wants to live. Melanie is working with her gifts. She's a natural salesperson and strong in relationship-building. Tiffany sees Melanie's lifestyle and wants it so bad for herself, she decides to get her real estate license. Now, there's nothing wrong with Tiffany wanting more from life and even wanting some of what her friend has. But Tiffany made the mistake of amounting Melanie's success and lifestyle to what she did for a living. Tiffany was so focused on Melanie's lifestyle and what she did

What happens when we are not walking in our purpose?

that she gave minimal thought or effort to her own gifts and how she could use them to build her own successful, fulfilling lifestyle. Again, Tiffany's gift is in teaching, and she loves kids. She has everything it takes to open her own Learning Center, enabling her to walk in her own gifts of teaching and working with kids, both at the same time. This would provide her so much joy and fulfillment and possibly enable her to achieve all she wanted that she's now pursuing in a field that doesn't align with her strengths. Do you see how placing your value in others can work against you? How placing your identity in others can derail your own success in finding your purpose? We all have our own gifts and talents that can serve us once we make the decision to utilize them to our advantage. It is vital for us to hold true our own identity and not be lost in the success or the identity of others.

Job to job

Have you ever met that individual who is doing something different every time you speak with them? Today they are a contractor, last week they were in sales, three months ago they were doing overseas work and just a year ago they were excited about a new network marketing company. These individuals are constantly moving from job to job, from career to career, from business to business, having new

What happens when we are not walking in our purpose?

experiences, searching for the one thing they just can't seem to grasp the answer to, "what was I created to do?" A person that doesn't know why they were created will find themselves doing anything and everything but that. They're on a constant search seeking to find who they are. The moment they come across a new opportunity to where it sounds like they can benefit financially, off they go. Unfortunately, through all these different endeavors, they rarely find fulfillment. Even if they acquire a massive amount of success and money, they still feel a void that has not yet been filled, and they often end up leaving that field abruptly. It's very possible this person hasn't taken the time to ask themselves the questions that matter most regarding their profession and well-being. They are literally going through life unfulfilled and unsatisfied. They wake up every day to a job they're not excited about going to because they are chasing profit, not purpose. They are on the lookout for pay, not provision. They often find themselves at a job that gives them nothing more than a consistent paycheck, no lasting sense of joy or impact. They often do no more work than necessary but just enough to not get fired. The job then pays them just enough that they keep coming back, though unfulfilled. The job-to-job cycle is hard to break unless a person becomes fed up. They have to get to the point where they're sick and tired of being sick and tired. The need for something

What happens when we are not walking in our purpose?

more, something different, becomes so great that they are willing to even sacrifice pay for peace. This person is *now* ready for fulfillment. The problem is, most don't even know where to start looking. They have no answer for their issue. In fact, many can't even pinpoint the issue. They just know they are very unhappy and unfulfilled. This book just might be the answer they've been looking for.

We settle

What comes to mind when I say the word, Superman? Would it be his laser vision, the fact that he's faster than a speeding bullet, superhuman strength, ability to see through people and objects, or maybe his ability to fly? All of these abilities can also be looked at as gifts. What if I were to tell you that you are Superman or Superwoman? You also have gifts, talents, and abilities. I remember when I made the decision to quit my job. It was shortly after I had just seen a photo of Superman. He was in chains and surrounded by two guards. I never forgot how I felt when I saw this photo. I almost felt like I was looking at myself. Here was Superman with all these gifts, talents, and abilities, and here he was in chains and bondage. All of his potential was useless. Seeing this photo made me look at where I was in my life from a whole new perspective. Here I was, this young,

What happens when we are not walking in our purpose?

vibrant, enthusiastic, motivated, inspired person with all these gifts and talents being unused or limited by my choice to continue working where I was. I decided I would no longer allow it to hold me back from reaching my full potential. I decided I would step out on faith and find a way to utilize these talents of mine. I wasn't sure exactly how, but I knew it's what I wanted and what I was going to chase until I found it.

We all know that as powerful as Superman is, He also has an energy source from which he draws his power, the sun. As long as the sun is up and out, Superman can be all that he needs to be to keep his planet safe with the use of his powers. But he also has a weakness, kryptonite. All of the power that's within him, all of the abilities that he has become useless when he's around Kryptonite. Too many of us focus too much attention on our kryptonite. We focus on our weaknesses and what we can't do or have not done instead of drawing power and inspiration from our "son," which are things and people that inspires, motivate, and ignites us.

We miss out on life-changing opportunities

A video went viral of Adrien Broner at a fast-food restaurant. The famous boxer walked in with $10,000 cash and told an employee it was theirs to have if

What happens when we are not walking in our purpose?

they quit their job right there on the spot. The initial employee that he proposed the offer to did not accept. They missed out on $10,000 cash to keep a job that paid them a minimum wage salary. What do you think was going through that person's mind? What would you have done? Would you have taken the money and ran? What do you think could have been the hesitance for why that employee did not take the money? When we don't know why we were created and don't have a plan set for our lives, we miss out on life-changing opportunities that can aid to propel us to where we want to be. I strongly believe that the employee did not take the money because they had no idea what to do next. They probably thought to themselves, "If I take this money, I have no job...then what?" If that is the case, they chose to see the glass half empty by focussing on what they would lose and not on what they would gain. Fear held them back. They had no purpose, no vision, no direction as to where to go next, so they stayed put, in their comfortable position. When you have a purpose that you are aware of and opportunities arise, you are in a better position to take hold and grab those opportunities.

We fall into peer pressure

Johnny and Jason are two teenagers from the same neighborhood with the same family background.

What happens when we are not walking in our purpose?

Both Johnny and Jason are raised in a single-parent household in 3rd ward, Houston, TX. Johnny has a dream and goal to make it to the NBA and is currently playing on his high school's team. Jason has no idea what he would like to do and is just in school because that's where he's supposed to be, and that's where his friends are. Both Johnny and Jason get approached by other young men in their age group about engaging in other extracurricular activities with gang affiliation. Johnny doesn't even have to think about his answer; he knows that this direction can ultimately derail his possibility of making it to the NBA. On the other hand, Jason has no goals, no destination, no vision, and no one seeking interest to find out what he wants in life. So it's easier for him to respond, "What the heck? I have nothing better to do." Now, both of these men grew up in the same situation and have the same opportunities, but one went left, the other right. Why? When you have a vision and know where you want to go, you know what roads will not take you there. No matter how young you are, your mind should be filled with thoughts, ideas on how you can reach your goal and how you want it to look once you've obtained it. Even as adults, similar occurrences take place all the time. Lack of vision derails them from a past they would have otherwise chosen. Whether it becomes a constant cycle of meaningless drinking, partying, hanging out, etc., without a purpose, your focus is limited, leaving you open to an array of opportunities, many of which won't serve you.

Midlife crises

The compulsion to change your life completely or make drastic decisions once you reach a certain age can be considered a midlife crisis. People in this situation may find themselves trying to relive their younger years by getting involved in adrenaline rush activities, impulse buying, making attempts to look younger, or sometimes boredom and depression. It doesn't affect everyone the same way, but there is a major change from how this person generally is. This can stem from the constant thought of getting older, life passing them by and they're unsure how to deal with it. They lack a sense of purpose to know what they should be focusing on, working towards and how to go about the day by day of their lives. They are soul searching, often feeling unhappy, unfulfilled, and frustrated with life that they feel they may receive some fulfillment by suddenly making some drastic change or changes. They are unsettled and uneasy about life. They question why they are here and what's next. The constant change is an outside action to an internal problem, lack of purpose, and direction. Going through this crisis often causes many individuals to take a major hit to their savings

What happens when we are not walking in our purpose?

accounts. Psychological warfare enables them to rationalize making big purchases which can happen quite often. They often don't realize the financial damage that's been done. Sometimes they may even cut off old long-term friends around the same age group, trying to disconnect from being reminded that they're getting older. This person seeks to find fulfillment to fill a void that can only be satisfied by walking in their purpose.

"To the degree that you don't follow your passion and purpose, you'll end up working for someone who did."
~ unknown

CHAPTER 4

How do you find your purpose?

How do you find your purpose?

Did you know there's a difference between looking and seeking? Looking is to glance in the direction of. But seeking is to make an actual attempt to find. To find your purpose, one must seek it out. Seeking takes diligence and effort. When seeking, I believe that there are four main elements that, when they are put together and utilized at the same time, a new revelation unfolds. I implore you to not only read and understand these four concepts but *apply* them. Your purpose is to find your way. One of the things I like to say is, use 'triple A' to find your way: Awareness, Acceptance, and Application. Once you become *aware* of these four concepts, *accept* them and *apply* them. Remember, effort must be used in applying. Let's dig in!

Pay attention

I believe the first step to real change in any area is awareness. How can you change something that you're not aware of? To find your purpose, you really have to pay attention to what's going on. Pay attention to your thoughts, your feelings, your emotions, your actions, and your experiences. Take a look at the world around you, how you interact with it, and how it interacts. Be aware of how others respond to you in certain situations and environments. Know, and keep in mind that in life, we all experience patterns. For instance, is there a compliment on something that you do that you seem to get regularly and consistently? Have you recognized this pattern or constantly dismissing it?

In my personal life, I started to pay attention when I heard numerous times that others listened when I started to speak. When I spoke on different platforms, I started hearing that people would want to hear what I had to say. I started realizing that after I spoke, people would often walk up to me after the session and ask me questions and learn more about who I was, what I did, where, and how I obtained my knowledge. Random strangers from all walks of life, various backgrounds, and all age groups were interested in what I had to say and connecting with me beyond that setting. Whether I was at church, a classroom, in open discussions, going out in public, or even in group settings, people just genuinely seemed interested in hearing what I had to say. But I literally didn't realize this or notice it until I started to pay attention. Once others made me aware, I could no longer proceed like I had not heard it before. It probed the part of the brain known as the reticular activating system, that enables us to consciously become more aware of specifics. I started to really pay attention.

It's possible others have been telling you your purpose, but you weren't paying attention. Let this be the moment that you decide to pay attention to where

How do you find your purpose?

you're going right now in life and what's taking place. If you were to continue the same path that you're on right now, where will you be in five years? How about in 10 years? 20 years? If you keep doing what you're doing right now, would you be happy with your life twenty years from now? If not, what changes need to be made to where you will be pleased with the results? What are you doing to change the course of direction if that's needed? Who do you have in your life paying attention to your actions that lead to your results? Are you paying for, or do you have a coach, a mentor, or an advisor? Do you have somebody in your life who has reached some of the goals you desire and are you learning from that individual? All of the clients I have now have reached out to me and expressed that they desire to receive some of the results I've obtained and achieved. Whether it be from mindset or physical achievement, there is something in me that they saw and want for themselves. But they were paying attention to their results and realized that they could achieve more and weren't living to their full potential. Be careful not to pay attention to what others have but the results that they receive, consistently. Are you paying attention to your results, and are you happy with them? Are you feeling fulfilled in what you do now?

To find your purpose, pay attention to your patterns, thoughts, feelings, emotions, and actions that all lead to your results. Pay attention to your thoughts and know that your thoughts affect your feelings and your feelings affect your thoughts, and they both affect your actions, which ultimately leads to your results. Read that again. Both current results and past, pay attention to your experiences, encounters, and interactions. Pay attention to your current path and determine where it may lead you if you continue to follow where you're going and ask yourself, "Is that where I really want to be?" Pay attention to the success and even failures around you. Make a decision right now to accept your past failures as something to learn from; they are lessons. The blessing is in the lesson if you've paid attention. You didn't lose, you LEARNED.

It's also important to know that you don't have to go through something, personally, to get the lesson. Robert Kiyosaki said, "Everyone is a mentor. You can learn from everyone. You can learn from one person what to do and from another person what not to do." Either way, if you're paying attention, you get the lesson. This is why it can be so powerful to get around other individuals that have gone where you're going. Learn from their experiences and failures. You can save yourself some time and some trouble by being able to take detours (not short-cuts), just from learning from others.

Similarly, I also heard the inspirational rapper Keith Wallace say, "A man learns from his mistakes, but a wise man learns from the mistakes of others." As long as you get the lesson, that's all that matters. It doesn't matter how you get it; just make sure you get it.

If you haven't been paying attention, there are tools that you can use to do so that will raise your level of awareness which can then increase your chances of learning your purpose. One of the tools that I have used and one that I stress my clients to use is explained in my free ebook that can be found at PurposeForMeBonus.com.

Take advantage of this free information and put it to use in your own life.

Exposure

Is it possible to be or do something you have not seen? How can you? How can you participate in something you have no knowledge of? Therefore, to find your purpose, you must expose yourself to new ideas, new experiences, and new events. Sometimes this exposure will be from new activities that you partake in. Other exposure could be hearing about what others have done. I remember speaking in the school system to elementary, middle, and even high school students. I would love to see their faces light

How do you find your purpose?

up when I tell them what it is that I do for a living. Some of them had no knowledge that real estate or speaking was an option to choose as a career path. But once they learned, they were intrigued. They were exposed to something new and, therefore, excited about the possibilities now open to them. I think it's vitally important for our youth and even adults to indulge in new activities, trying new things, going to new places that even seem uncomfortable from the outside looking in. Doing so will place us in a situation to possibly discover new gifts, talents, or skills we never knew we had.

I remember when I first discovered I had a gift for writing poetry. I was in high school and had very strong feelings for my high school sweetheart. I wanted to do something nice for her but something different. So I decided to write to her. I never really attempted to write poetry before, but I found it easy to make the words rhyme. Before I knew it or realized what I was doing, I had a poem before my eyes. I was shocked about this newfound skill but also excited at the same time. I found myself writing poetry for different events, on different topics, and it just came so easily. I then began to perform some of my pieces at church functions. I literally put myself out there to try something new and realized I had the gift of poetry. I could now say I'm a poet, but only because I took the chance to try something new outside of my

How do you find your purpose?

comfort zone. To this day, my high school sweetheart still has poetry that I wrote for her 20 years ago. Both her life and mine were forever impacted by my one decision to step out and try something new.

Yes, it's true. Exposure can be scary because sometimes it forces us to leave our comfort zone. But at the same time, it's possible we might never truly find success and fulfillment until we're able to do so. Just like love requires vulnerability, finding your purpose requires new experiences, many of which can be found outside of your comfort zone. Everything you want in life can be found outside of your comfort zone. You must grow to the person that can achieve, obtain and acquire that which you really desire. Exposure is one of the key factors to find out why you are really here and where you're gifted.

One of the things that I encourage my clients to expose them to if they haven't already is the power of solitude and silence. It can be very beneficial to be in a space where the only voice you can hear would be your own or God's. Know that God often speaks in silence and solitude. When no one else is around is when you can hear from Him. Take, for instance, when God gave Moses his purpose. Notice that God did not speak to Moses through the burning bush until He got him alone. How often do you spend time alone, awake, in silence, and expecting to receive instructions and insight?

Reflecting on the past

Reflection is a very powerful step in finding out your purpose. Doing so effectively allows you to see things from an outside perspective versus a first-person perspective while you're experiencing it. Looking back on past experiences may allow you to see things from a different viewpoint than you might have seen previously. Remember, you see things as you continue to grow. Regret is a reflection of the past. It's looking back at something you've done (or didn't do) and wishing you would have done things differently, but that's only because now you see it from a different perspective, one that's different from when you made the decision at the moment.

One of the biggest decisions of my professional life that I would often reflect on was my decision to no longer continue real estate full time for a time period. I obtained my license in 2004 after the suggestion from Step-Father. My mother owned her own Mortgage Company, for which my stepfather works with her. He thought it would make sense for me to obtain my license and keep the money in the family. I would sell the houses; they do the loans. So that's what we did as a family business. Around 2008, the market crashed, and my mother lost her business. The realtor mentoring me gave me the option to continue working with him by being an assistant at

How do you find your purpose?

his home office. He was doing quite well in real estate, but I had never worked in an office before, so I chose to leave the industry. He later became the number one real estate agent in the city, and I often wondered what would have happened and what would I have learned had I chosen to stay. But I also realize why I made the decision to leave...I was influenced by the opinions and thought processes of others and what they said about the market. Had I known then, what I know now, I would have made a completely different decision. This type of reflection is vital to my understanding of who I am and why I made the decisions that I made. Understanding who I am is necessary to help me understand why I'm here and why I was created. Reflecting on circumstances and situations where I had a high level of emotions (high or low) is also very helpful in understanding myself. These realizations and observations help me see how I think and how I respond. It helps me now to realize my mindset from then and helps me make better decisions going forward.

When it comes to reflection, you don't want to just look at things that took place in your adult life. Go back further, even look at things that happened to you when you were a child and even through your youth. Remember that as you take a look at events that occurred then and you see them now, you see them differently than when you were experiencing them at that moment. Reflect on your feelings and emotions, then ask yourself would you feel the same way going through the same experiences now? Would you even make some of the same decisions now? Try not to place your mind in a state of regret but in the state of awareness of observations. This reflection helps you better see patterns in your life. Now that you are aware, you can now break these patterns, if you need to.

Asking questions

There's a famous saying: never answer a question with a question. Well, in this situation, I think the best way to find the answer to this question of what my purpose is, is by asking more and different questions. Now that you understand that reflecting on the past, exposure, and paying attention are vital keys to finding one's purpose, you also want to be certain to ask yourself the right questions. Asking questions opens the mind and probes it to look for answers. But of course, the right questions must be asked for this process to be effective. What happens to a student in the classroom setting that's learning something new and never asks any questions? Will he or she truly get a real understanding as to what's being taught? Will they really learn all there is to know about the current subject at hand? Well, guess what, YOU are your biggest test. YOU are your biggest subject. YOU ought to know yourself better than anyone else. But do you? Asking yourself the right questions on a regular and consistent basis probes the mind to constantly look for answers even when you're not even paying attention. Your brain is meant to be programmed. To the degree that you don't program your mind yourself, it will be programmed for you as a result of your neglect. Your mind is programmed with repetition, consciously and subconsciously.

Apart from asking yourself the right questions, you also want to ask others, those individuals you deem to be living a life of fulfillment and walking in their purpose. How did they get there? What path did they take? What obstacles did they overcome?

What I've learned is that asking questions takes humility. It takes a humble state of mind to place yourself in a position to ask a question because what you're saying is, I don't know. Who wants to admit that they don't know something? Your pride must be laid aside to ask questions. How many times have you been in a classroom session and were glad someone asked a question that you thought of, but didn't ask? Why didn't you ask? Chances are, you didn't want others to know what you didn't know. When you start asking questions, some of the answers will come immediately, others you may have to sit and ponder. All this will take some reflection and a deeper observation to find the answer. But if you seek, you shall find. The problem is most people don't seek. They only take a quick glance, and when the answer is not staring them in their face immediately, they move on. Diligence is the key in this process.

In my coaching program, I go through a plethora of specific questions that each individual must ask themselves to find out their specific purpose. Some of these questions you may have thought about and others you may not have. The difference is, now that you have been opened up to the idea of asking the questions along with reflecting, new exposure, and paying attention, you may now be in a better position to understand yourself and why you were created. Remember, you understand things better and more as you continue to grow. Your level of understanding is different, as you are a different person.

Chapter 5

Why is our purpose not for us?

Why is our purpose not for us?

Does it seem interesting to you that something that is "yours" isn't even for you? Does that even make any sense? I believe it's all perception; it all depends on how you look at things. Have you ever considered who gave it to you? In this chapter, I'll be discussing one perception of seeing our purpose as being for others, not ourselves.

Your purpose is for others and the world

I heard the famous John Maxwell make a statement I've never forgotten. He said, "Success is for you, but significance is for others." Wow. What a statement. How many people deem themselves successful? Or how many others deem another person's success by their own standards, from the outside looking in? But what is successful? Is that by accumulating monetary gain? I, personally, would rather focus my attention on the success of others. Impact. Making a difference in the lives of others. Jim Rohn said, "To get what you want, help enough people get what they want. If you want to make a million dollars, help a million people." To me, service is the way to success. Even in my profession as a realtor. Many would call me a salesperson, but I like to that of myself as a servant. I'm here to serve those that I work with and work for. It's all perception.

Why is our purpose not for us?

As the person who gets excited about seeing and hearing about other people reach and walk in their purpose and full potential, I find myself asking people about their purpose fairly often. Unfortunately, most of the people that I ask have no idea. Those that do have an idea always tend to give me relatively the same answer. They say, "I believe my purpose is to help people." Well yeah, your purpose is to help others. But what does that mean? The question is, in what way? *How* are you helping these individuals? What are you helping them do, be, understand or overcome? When a person states their purpose, it should be specific. Everyone's purpose on this Earth involves the betterment of other individuals around them. We are all here for one another. Nothing that you do, no gift or service that you provide and utilize can be maximized to its full potential to benefit just yourself. It will always be for the edification of others. Your purpose is not for you because it's to uplift, encourage, educate, inspire, teach, build others outside of yourself. Think of the most successful person or even the most influential. Is it safe to say that this person is walking in their purpose? Let's just say, for one example, one of the most successful people was Steve Jobs. I think we can all agree that he is mounted to a massive degree of success. He's made a fortune with his creation...his purpose. But who benefited? Was it just him? Imagine if he kept

Why is our purpose not for us?

his purpose to himself. The whole world would have been deprived of his genius creation in Apple. So, in a sense, keeping your purpose to yourself or not placing yourself in a position to find out your purpose can actually be selfish. You're doing yourself and the world a disservice by not walking in your purpose. You're depriving the world of your gift, service, or wisdom. The world was supposed to be changed for the better because you were here. You were created to do something massive, something important, something special that can change the lives of one or many. But if you have no idea what that is, is that fair to those you were *supposed* to touch? I personally believe that this book will touch and inspire millions. I believe that this book will sell millions of copies and be converted to 30 + languages around the world. This book will change many lives and open the eyes of so many to see the possibilities of those with no idea where to begin finding their purpose. Me creating this book and creating a platform to teach these ideas is me walking in my purpose. And because I am walking in mine, now others can walk in theirs. Again, we all benefit from each other. What is a pastor without a congregation to serve and lead? What is a speaker without a crowd or audience to speak to? What is a doctor without a patient to cure? What is a teacher without a student to teach? Who is your favorite vocalist? What if they never follow their passion and purpose to pick up the microphone and sing? Would it matter how well they could sing if no one heard them? How many lives would *not* have been touched by their musical message? Your purpose was designed to bless others. You receive fulfillment, and they receive your gift.

Your purpose is for God

Think of your purpose as your gift from God. I believe the most effective way to use your gift is to give it back to him. You give it back to him by using it amongst his children. Although our gifts come from God, it is our responsibility to seek them out, cultivate them and use them. Remember that gifts usually come wrapped. When someone hands you a gift, do you know what it is? You don't, but how do you find out? When you receive a gift, it's expected for you to unwrap the gift. How would you feel if you gave someone a gift and they never used it? Or even worse, how would you feel if you gave someone a gift and they never even unwrapped it? You literally took the time, energy, and thought process it takes to put together a gift and then additional time to wrap the gift for the person that you give it to, not even to open it. How do you think God feels? God has given something specifically for you with the expectation that you would take the initiative in doing what is necessary to find out exactly what it is. Then He's hoping that you would be grateful and care enough about the gift to cultivate it and use it. Whether that gift is to sing, dance, encourage, teach, serve, or athletic ability, it's up to you to unwrap it.

There comes a point in every parent's process of rearing children where they must allow the child to figure some things out on their own. This is the only way the child can continue to grow without being completely dependent. It's a parent's job to provide and protect the child up until a certain point. Parents are to raise the child by building a solid foundation. Once that foundation is built, slowly, the child Is expected to become more and more self-sufficient. Do you remember the relationship between the Creator and the creation in chapter one? Although those that use the creation benefit, it also benefits the Creator. Any creator wants to see its creation being utilized and maximize to its full potential. Can you imagine creating something that no one ever uses? All that time invested, ideas acted out, for creating something that was never put to use. This was never meant to be for you and me. Your creator gave you the gift so that you can be a blessing to His people, and He can receive a return on His time invested. You are valuable to Him and the world. Not discovering your gift or not using your gift is a disservice to the world.

Your position and purpose makes you more effective

I remember hearing about a story of a basketball coach that did an experiment with his team to make a point. He took the five best players of the team and placed them together on team A. Then, he took the bench players and placed them together to make Team B. Then, he told both teams that team A would play Team B in the scrimmage game. Team A laughed and scoffed, knowing that this was going to be too easy. Team B looked at each other confused, knowing they had no chance, but, as competitors, they were still up for the challenge. Then, the coach decided to make a stipulation for the game. He said the players of team A would not be allowed to play their natural positions. The center will play the point guard position, and the shooting guard will play power forward. This stipulation changed the game drastically. In the end, the less talented team B triumphed over team A. This taught the players of both teams a valuable lesson, and the coach stressed the point of the exercise: no matter how good you are, you can only be your best and most effective playing your position.

In life, your position is your purpose. The position that you were created for is the area you were called to be using your gifts, your talents, and that which you are passionate about. Being out of position or alignment with our purpose leads to frustration, dysfunction, and unfulfillment. We must make it a point to be the most effective we can be in our lives. We must place ourselves in situations and circumstances that allow us to reach our full potential and maximize ourselves, allowing others to benefit from our actions. There is a sense of fulfillment we receive when we are effective in what we do. Every human being is built with the desire to feel important, to feel valued, to feel useful, and to feel wanted. Children act out at school and home *just* to get attention from those that they love. They desire to be valued, feel like they belong, and that their presence is needed. Even as adults, we never lose that desire because we were created with that in us. The desire to feel loved and appreciated is our greatest desire as humans.

Life in one word

If you would take life and sum it up in one word, what would that word be? One word for me to describe life would be "love". Remember that God created life, and God is love. I have a saying: Life in one word is love, and the best way to show love is to give. So, therefore, we should live to give.

Meaning of Life
To give or not to give, that is the question

Why is our purpose not for us?

The reason for our existence & purpose, what is the lesson
Accumulate, acquire, achieve and obtain
Is what society tells us, forced thoughts on our brain
They say you are what you have & what you have is who you are
But I'm here to tell you, suppress those thoughts and raise the bar.
What is the meaning of life, the reason why we're here
Why do we chase meaningless things that won't matter in a year
What does it profit a man to gain the world and lose his soul
To the man who dies with more riches than his life could hold
It is better to give than receive, I believe
How much of what we gain can we take when we leave
I submit to you today life's a puzzle and we're the pieces
Each one of your gifts are the edges to fill the creases
You have the cure for my disease and I have the book for your potential
Write the vision, make it plain, grab the paper, where's the pencil
I've learned that my past, wisdom, experience, and knowledge

Why is our purpose not for us?

Expressed justly for you can be more beneficial than college
Young man, read my lips, heed my words, hear my voice
Turn around, don't look back...don't make my same bad choice
You see I've been there and done that, I've tried it all before you
Learn from my mistakes, I've walked this past so you won't have to
Each one teach one, there's more than enough for us all to do.
Unity is the answer, held together with love
Giving is the action, like God's son from above
Life in one word is LOVE....amongst the living
Love expressed outwardly thru the action of giving
Your thoughts, ideas, time, love, advice and skills
Giving of yourself can pay more than just the bills
And so with that said, I'll leave you all with this
Story, and hope you'll find the meaning of life and not miss...

After his death
They found a little paper in his belongings that read
His mission and purpose for his life and it said,
"I'll spend the first half of my life making a fortune in pay
The second half of my life, I'll spend giving it all away"

Why is our purpose not for us?

And just what he wrote is EXACTLY what he lived
Andrew Carnegie was his name; he made a fortune just to give

What comes to mind when you read my poem on the meaning of life? Do you agree with it? Have you ever sat and thought, what IS the meaning of life? Not just your life, but life in general. Why *are* we here? Why did God create us? More specifically, why did God create YOU?

Chapter 6

How to confirm we are walking in our purpose

How to confirm we are walking in our purpose

Let's say you've been going through the action steps outlined in this book, and you've narrowed down what you think your purpose might be. Or you've been walking in an area that you believe might be your purpose. You have a pretty good idea, but you'd like to confirm it. Well, how do you do so? In this chapter, we will be discussing some of the things that you can be sure to look out for to confirm you may be walking in your purpose.

Passion

Do you have a burning desire to continue doing what you're doing, and is it providing fulfillment, a joy you receive when indulging in it? One of the ways to confirm we are walking in our purpose is by asking ourselves if this is something we're passionate about. Passion is very important because it allows us to push through hardship and obstacles that may arise in the things that we do and in our chosen path. Passion can be displayed as excitement, joy, enthusiasm, and an overall burning desire and love for what we're doing. Do you look forward to the next time that you get to do it again? Are you looking for ways to improve and make it better, or does it feel like work or a chore to you? If you clearly have a passion for a particular area, that *can* possibly be an indication of something that may be an area of your purpose.

How to confirm we are walking in our purpose

As for me, if I'm sitting in a classroom and a discussion is taking place about a subject that I feel confident and knowledgeable about, it is extremely difficult, almost torture, for me not to be able to share my insight. I feel as if I just must be able to share once the opportunity arises. I am unapologetically raising my hand to provide additional feedback questions or alternative answers to what was just stated. It even bothers me when a teacher is explaining something to a student, and they're explaining it in such a way that I know the student will not understand completely based on their method. I can hardly tolerate poor teaching being taught in my presence. That irks me; it really grinds my gears, and so I would have to speak up. I'm passionate about helping others grasp an understanding because my gift is in teaching. So, I'm naturally able to explain things so that they can be understood by most, maybe not everyone, but most. You could say I'm passionate about teaching. Your passion is something that you love to do, especially when the opportunity presents itself. You get this feeling, this urge, and excitement to do it, and you'll do it for free, just for the love of it. Professional athletes start off playing their prospective sport as kids who just played it because they loved it. They were just passionate and excited to be playing. Making money to do so wasn't even a thought. Passion drives you to want to do more of what you love.

How to confirm we are walking in our purpose

Now along with this, we have to keep in mind, though, that passion is one of those things that we really have to be careful with. While it's true we want to make sure that we're passionate about what we're doing, we still want to keep in mind that it is possible to be passionate about something that we're not good at or that may not be our purpose. Yes, it's true. We can even find joy and fulfillment in some areas where we're not gifted. I'll give you an example: have you ever watched American Idol? I think it's clear and safe to say that many of the individuals that attended tryouts are extremely passionate about singing. Even some of those with the most vigor, excitement, energy, and passion have absolutely no talent in that area. I mean, these people are on National Television yelling out a horrific tune at the top of their lungs and we're here wondering where are their real friends? No shame. No hesitation. No fear. No problem. While it's apparent and unfortunate that they don't seem to have any real friends or family to tell them the truth, these people are still chasing that dream and passionate about what they're doing that probably isn't their purpose. But you have to give them their props for courage and for stepping out on faith and in their dreams. So, when participating in things that we are passionate about, we also want to pay attention to how others respond to us. It's okay to ask others their honest opinion about what we're doing. It can also be helpful to have that brutally honest friend who doesn't mind telling you even what you don't want to hear. You know that friend that barely has a filter? Call them up and ask them, "Should I be doing this?" Or "Am I good at this?" Be passionate, but also be good.

People

I said it before, and I'll say it again, your purpose is not for you; it is for others. So, when looking at your purpose and what you are doing, ask yourself, who benefits from this? Whose life is being transformed, changed, uplifted? Not only will our purpose benefit others, but it can often take others to help us walk in our purpose. Is there anyone assisting or encouraging you in that particular area? Are they displaying their faith in what you do and offering their support? Others around us often confirm what we should be doing, but again, we must be paying attention to see it. Sometimes, other people see what's in us before we see what's in us. We can often be our worst critics. This can make it difficult to see ourselves for who we really are. What's also important to understand about people is that not everybody is for you. This is a lesson that I had to learn myself. It took me a minute to grasp. I just couldn't understand. At one point in my life, I got addicted to personal development. I would spend hours upon hours and days listening to the world's most highly sought-after motivational speakers and influencers. Anywhere from Tony Robbins, to John Maxwell, to Les Brown, to Zig Ziglar, to Bob Proctor, Eric Thomas, the list goes on and on. A couple of times, a person would ask me who I listen to that I draw motivation from. I would gladly mention one of these names, KNOWING this person would feel the same way I do about them. But surprisingly, sometimes, that wasn't the case. Sometimes, a person would have something negative to say about somebody on this list. This happened multiple times. In my mind, these people were so awesome that I thought everybody else would think they were just as awesome as I did, but that wasn't so. But it taught me a lesson. And this is why we must all find our own lane. We can both talk about the same thing, but how I deliver it can be completely different from how you deliver it, and we will both draw different audiences based on how we deliver it. We all have a specific audience based on who we are, personally. For instance, Tony Robbins and Gary Vee are known for giving powerful talks that include a lot of foul, adult language. To one individual, that's a turnoff they choose not to engage in. But another person loves it. They love the raw, uncensored, uncut, direct energy. Different people also receive the same information different, based on where they are in thei lives. What a realization this was for me. No matter what you do, you have a specific audience. You have certain individuals designated for you to touch. You are not meant to save everyone, nor should you try to. If you want to live a short life, try to save everyone. Knowing and understanding this relieves massive pressure for you to go out and be who you were called to be; do what you were called to do. Only engage and release energy in those individuals that you feel are for you. You will know them. They will be thankful and grateful for you and your gift. There will always be others that will not understand who you are and what you do, and that's okay. They weren't meant to understand. Focus your attention on those that do.

Pleasing

I stated earlier in the book that I often ask people what do they feel their purpose is? Their response is usually, "To help people." It's a generic response, but it's also a sincere one. But it also does not come as a surprise because I believe most people generally want to help others. We all want to make a difference. We all want to impact, inspire, encourage or be a blessing on some level. Yes, it's true, some of us have to dig deeper than others, and some have suppressed this desire, or it's hidden behind hurt, disappointment, and even trauma, but I believe it's there. I think we were created with a desire to be this way. We want for others what we typically want for ourselves. We can all relate with some of our core values because deep down, we all want the same thing: to be healthy, wealthy, and feel loved and appreciated. If I were to ask you, do you want these aspects of life for yourself? Do you want to be healthy? Would you like to be wealthy or financially comfortable? How would you view life if you didn't feel loved or appreciated? None of us want to live in sickness, and none of us want to live in poverty. It's hard to enjoy life when you're constantly experiencing lack or need. Being in a state of need causes frustration, discord, dissension, and stress. So, when you're doing what you love, without the stress of health or finances, life is beautiful and pleasing. So, what happens when we do fulfill this desire to be a blessing to others? Once you begin walking in your purpose, you are making an impact in the lives of others. This impact gives you a strong sense of fulfillment. It's pleasing to your soul. It fills a void within you that nothing else can fill. A perfect example of this would be in the famous Bible story of Cain and Abel. In the Book of Genesis, Cain, the Firstborn of Adam and Eve, killed his younger brother Abel because of jealousy. Cain Was a farmer whose punishment from God, along with being driven from God's presence, was to no longer reap the benefit from the crops he planted. Now the Bible doesn't say a whole lot about Cain, but from this, we can gather that Cain must have really loved what he did because his response to God was, "My punishment is too much for me to bear." Cain's work, his purpose, was so pleasing to him that he could not bear the thought of not doing it or seeing the harvest from his labor. Wow, that's fulfillment. But it's also confirmation. It's an indication that he was doing what he was supposed to be doing. He was doing what he was created to do. Your purpose should be pleasing. Without it, there will be a void.

> "When you work the ground, it will no longer yield its crops for you. You will be a Restless Wanderer on the Earth." Cain said to the Lord, " My punishment is more than I can bear."
> Genesis 4:12-13

Peace

Peace can be a major indication you are walking in your purpose. Now when I say peace, I'm not saying that everything will always be smooth sailing and straight paths. You are still going to have to work. You will still experience and go through some roadblocks, setbacks, and overcome many obstacles, but even still, you will have a sense of peace. You will know it. You will be able to feel it within you. Even through the

How to confirm we are walking in our purpose

midst of a storm and a rocky situation of you walking in your purpose, you will still have peace at times. When all else fails, follow peace. Peace is calmness. It's a sense of inner knowing that things will work out, that you are being kept, that God is in control, and that you are where you're supposed to be.

There was a time in my life when I was sleeping in my car. I had all my possessions in the back seat and the trunk. I would wake up in the mornings, drive to the gym to shower, brush my teeth, change and head to Starbucks or Panera Bread to work for the day. It was a very humbling experience to sell homes when I had no home. I did this for months, but throughout the process, I had a sense of peace. Sometimes, God will allow situations to take place where no one can help you but Him. I just knew this was only for a time frame and that this season will be over soon enough. So, I didn't allow myself to stress or begin falling into any habits that didn't serve me because I knew this would only be a part of my story. If I continue walking, progressing, and being persistent, things would eventually change for me. I just knew it. They had to. Peace kept me and because I knew it, because I persisted, what I knew eventually came true. It was all a test, and you can't have TESTimony without the word "test."

In life, we all go through things to where we can't always see the end result. You have an idea of how you want it to end, but you may not be able to see it clearly. Having a sense of peace gives you clarity of mind, and comfort to still progress because there's an inner sense of just knowing it will work out in your favor. People have been known to quit jobs, demote themselves from positions, sever relationships, pay a little extra for an item or service just to have a sense of peace. I strongly believe that peace is priceless. At all costs, protect your peace.

"Finally, brothers, rejoice. Aim for restoration, comfort one another, agree with one another, live in peace; and the God of love and peace will be with you."
~ 2 Corinthians 13:11

Profit

There's a famous Bible verse that says your gift will make room for you. Your gift can also make room for opportunities that lead to your bank account. People will pay you for your gift. The question is, have you put a price on it? Whether your gift is speaking, teaching, providing hospitality, or some form of the arts, there are ways you can monetize it and yield a profit. I'm sure you know of individuals in all these fields. Some may be great at it, others you wonder what they're doing there, but they are getting paid in any case. It can be highly beneficial to place yourself

How to confirm we are walking in our purpose

around other individuals who share the same gifts and use them for their financial benefit. See how they are putting it to use, learn how they are cultivating it, read books on how to monetize it, and capitalize by making it something you do for others to benefit. Remember, your gift is an area that you're strong in, that others may be weak in. It comes naturally to you. People willingly pay for their weaknesses; they delegate them. It's a benefit to have you step in and fill the gap for the need to be met where they're weak or just lazy Lol. Even if it comes in the form of motivation from your knowledge, it's needed and highly sought-after. Even others with the same gift will need guidance, direction, mentorship, and a blueprint that you can provide. Make it a point to learn from others and even from yourself as you grow to cultivate your gift through the process of a plan of action and trial by error. It's possible that when you start walking in your gift, you may come across others that are walking in theirs, and you both have the opportunity to benefit from one another; you compensate for their weaknesses, and they compensate for yours equals a partnership or collaboration. This is powerful. Take this time to learn from one another and force each other to grow. Form and attend groups where everyone benefits by sharing content ideas, failures, experiences, and referrals. Masterminds are highly beneficial for networking and for cultivating new ideas among other like-minded individuals. The utilization of these groups can lead to you being more effective in your chosen field and purpose.

> "A man's gifts makes room for him, and brings him before Great Men."
> ~ Proverbs 18:16

CHAPTER 7

What to do when you find your purpose?

What to do when you find your purpose?

In this chapter, I'll be discussing what I suggest you should do once you discover your purpose. These are practical steps to follow. It's not enough to just know what you were created for. In life, it is not about what you know but what you *do* with what you know. Knowledge is obtaining information, but wisdom is having a deeper understanding of that knowledge through application and experience. As the book of Proverbs suggests, chose to use wisdom.

> Get wisdom, get understanding; do not forget my words or turn away from them. Do not forsake wisdom, and she will protect you; love her, and she will watch over you.
> ~ Proverbs 4:6-7

Get to work!!!

That about sums it up... get to work! Remember, you are held accountable for what you know. So, once you know better, you do better. Make it a point to live life on your terms by living for the purpose you were created. Expect to be satisfied, fulfilled, joyous, excited, and content once you begin to walk in it. Know that it won't be easy, but it'll definitely be worth it.

Plan

To be the most effective in what you're going to do and how you're going to do it, you need to develop a plan of action to follow. Simply put, plan your work, work your plan. This is a very simple formula for success in any area because those that fail to plan, plan to fail... by default. Some of the plans you form may come from your own thoughts based on what you've done in the past, ideas you may have had, or information you may have come across. Other parts of your plan may come from following a plan of action from those that have come before you, whether in the same field or even a different one. Yes, you can definitely learn from those in other fields, and I actually encourage you to look for ways to learn from others in different fields. In any case, you need to have a plan to follow. You need to know what you're going to do, how you're going to do it, what obstacles you may face, and what you may need to carry out this plan. One of the most important things to know and understand about a plan is that you don't know exactly how everything will play out once you put it into action. You can have the most perfect, well-thought-out plan, whether you devised it yourself or obtained it from somebody else, and it may not work out exactly how you planned or hoped it would. In fact, I can almost guarantee it won't. The moment you decide to make a life-changing decision, know that things will go wrong. Obstacles, setbacks, and roadblocks are inevitable. It's just a part of the process. No major success was met without failure and pushback. Therefore, your plan must constantly be tweaked, revised, altered, and refined until things slowly start to work out in your favor. You will not know what will work best for you until you put forth the effort and act on your plan. The inevitable success of the plan will be met, but not without execution, trial and error. Know this and accept it.

Remember, in chapter one, we talked about Dr. Myles Munroe's quote, "Your reason for existence is called purpose, and when you can see it, it's called vision?" Well, for that vision to be carried out, it must be mapped out and well planned. When I was in my early twenties, my stepfather gave me a poster with my favorite sport on it. But what really made it special was what the poster said towards the bottom: "A dream with a date becomes a goal. A goal broken down into steps becomes a plan. A plan backed by action makes that dream come true." WOW! What a statement. There is so much power stated in that quote. What if you actually turn your dreams and made them into goals to be carried out and chased until achieved? What if you achieved even half of your life's goals? What would your life look like then? Well, you can find out.

What to do when you find your purpose?

When planning, understand that it is a process and takes many hours of preparation and digging deep within oneself. Planning is hard work, which is part of the reason why most people never spend the time to do so. Most people never know where to start in planning their life. In my coaching program, we spend a couple of hours just planning. We go through a series of questions designed to help you pinpoint what is specifically for you. We make sure to map out what you want to achieve and how you are going to do so. Never forget that you can't be what you can't see. So, plan your work, work your plan.

> And the Lord answered me, and said, Write the vision, and make it plain upon tables, that he may run that readeth it. 3 For the vision is yet for an appointed time, but at the end, it shall speak, and not lie: though it tarry, wait for it; because it will surely come, it will not tarry.
> ~ Habakkuk 2:2-3 KJV

Protect

The law of use says that which you don't use, you lose. You protect your purpose by putting it to use. Understand that in life, you lose that which you don't use. If you possess or own something of value, and you leave it somewhere for any amount of time,

What to do when you find your purpose?

then you come back looking for it; more than likely, what has happened to it? It's gone. It now belongs to someone else. Yes, it was yours originally, but you didn't protect it. If you learn a new language and don't regularly or from time to time speak or practice that language, what happens to it? It's gone. You slowly lose the ability to speak it altogether. If you were to place your arm in a sling and leave it there for an extended amount of time, after too long, that arm would become useless. It's gone. Atrophy takes over. Do you see where I'm going with this? To maintain and protect a certain skill, task, or even sometimes your gift, you want to be sure to cultivate it and utilize it. This same principle also applies to your purpose. You have an opportunity. It's up to you to take advantage of it by grasping it. Remember, opportunities aren't lost; they go to someone else. How many times has an individual had an idea, hesitated to act on it, but then came across their idea acted upon from someone else who is now reaping the benefit? This happens all the time. It might have happened to you. Have you ever had a brilliant idea but never acted upon it? Then months, or even years later, you see that idea manifested? How did that make you feel? If it hasn't happened to you, can you imagine how that would feel? It's a terrible experience to have. The only way to prevent or avoid this experience is to act upon your ideas, your gifts, and your talents immediately. Protect them, for they are yours to have, but they're not yours to keep. I'm going to say that again to reiterate: it's yours to have, but it's not yours to keep. Opportunities will always go to someone. The question is, will that someone be you? Procrastination is a killer of purpose and dreams. Don't let your dreams die because you didn't have the faith in yourself or God to realize them. You were made to succeed. You were made to progress. You were made for a purpose and with a purpose. Your Creator makes no mistakes, and He didn't start with you.

Provide

How do you gauge how well you know something? Consider the idea that you've only learned something well enough to the degree you can teach it. Once you've been walking in your purpose for quite some time and it has become your expertise, in my opinion, it is also your responsibility to teach it to others. Remember that we are not the only ones that have this particular gift or passion. There will always be many others who share what you have but are unsure how to use it, much like how you were. I encourage you to take what you now know and seek to find these individuals. Make it a point to pass on your knowledge to those after you. The next generation needs to learn from your experiences. You can help them avoid some pitfalls because you've already been where they are or where they're going. This is why teaching, mentoring, and coaching are so important. Never forget where you came from. Remember, at one point, you had to be taught. Life is a cycle. Remain humble and give back. Take time out to share your experiences, your successes, your failures, your insight, and your time with others that will be glad to accumulate this knowledge. This can be done through providing mentoring programs, coaching platforms, hosting events, teaching classes, interviews, or just one-on-one interactions. However you decide to do so, make sure you provide a platform to share and teach what you know. It's up to you to decide whether or not you charge or do so for free. If it gets to the point you are devoting so much of your time to teaching and coaching, then at that point, it does make sense to be compensated for your time. But in the beginning stages, I suggest that you give the information for free, not looking for anything in return but the enjoyment of making a difference and impact. Just give because it's what you would have wanted coming from the other end. Remember when you were learning, you didn't always pay for the information you received, but you were grateful to receive it. Life is a cycle; you get back what you put out. The more you give, the more you get. Interestingly, once you start giving back, you start

What to do when you find your purpose?

finding yourself in positions to give even more. This is good. Take advantage of these opportunities. To get more for life, give more.

Conclusion

Congratulations!!! You finally made it. By now, you should know and hopefully understand some steps you can take to clarify how to find your purpose. Remember that people can only fully understand something when they're ready to receive it. So go back and read this book multiple times and at different stages of your life. Don't just read the information but make a conscious effort to apply it, act on it, put it to use, and watch how your life transforms for the better. God made you special. Therefore you cannot fail, you must succeed, but it takes faith and work together. Without work, faith is dead. You were born to win. He made you with your purpose, and your purpose is not for you. I love you.

Acknowledgements: Superstar Supporters

1. Rashid Tillis
2. Shannon Michelle Styles
3. Brook Burnside
4. Tray Smith
5. Tammie Lilly
6. Kenya Harris
7. Marie Guillory
8. Shani Arnold
9. Beverly Helms
10. Kristi Scott
11. Elyce Vardii
12. Tabitha Quinn
13. Nick Brown
14. Ilyasa Kennard
15. Oneida Williams
16. Joicelyn Robinson
17. Kenny Gransberry
18. Chris Webber
19. Julian Robinson
20. Ashley Dennis
21. Paul Garrett
22. Lillo Davis

Acknowledgements: Superstar Supporters

23. Rebecca Stewart
24. Renaldo Moore
25. Monica Collins
26. Shanisha Greer
27. Shawna Taylor
28. Autumn Ayri
29. Pam Clark
30. Donald Cyprian
31. Krystle Duncan
32. Kemesha Hall
33. Ladonna Landry
34. Taiese Nevels
35. Kesha Wattree
36. Kenny Jordan
37. Tavia Carter
38. Mia Icedo
39. Apache Goudeau
40. Richard Smith
41. Adrienne Phillips
42. Jason Boxie
43. Yolanda Wilkerson
44. Christie Williams
45. Anthony Austin
46. Tamarra Hamilton
47. Alyssa Dupiche
48. Jai Nelson
49. Julia McNeil
50. Lartrecia Kelley

Acknowledgements: Superstar Supporters

I'd like to acknowledge these superstar supporters as they were the first to support me in the pre-order of this book. For you to back your words with your actions and your finances without hesitation, truly warms my heart and I cherish our relationship.

Made in the USA
Middletown, DE
03 April 2024

52413778R00060